GOD HAD OTHER PLANS

GOD HAD OTHER PLANS

How I Overcame My Past
with the One Who Holds My Future

To order more copies of *God Had Other Plans*, contact the NCLL:
National Center for Life and Liberty
PO Box 270548
Flower Mound, TX 75027-0548
www.NCLL.org

Cindy McPherson is available for speaking engagements and will provide her audience with inspiration and hope.
To contact her, email *info@NCLL.org*.

God Had Other Plans: How I Overcame My Past with the One Who Holds My Future

Cover photo: *http://www.istockphoto.com/photo/family-hiking-in-the-mountains-21785668*
Cover photo title: Family Hiking in the Mountains
Design and page layout: AndrewRMinion Design (*http://andrewrminion.com*)

Unless otherwise notated, all Scripture quotations are from the New Living Translation.

Printed in the United States of America.

First Printing, 2015.

ISBN 978-0692381571

Dedication

I dedicate this book of difficult but important life lessons to my husband Scott, my daughter Marija Christine, and my mom.

Scott, my soul mate: when I met you, I found me. You encouraged me, inspired me, and truly loved me through the good times and the bad. You not only loved me, but you loved Marija like she was your own—unconditionally. I am so blessed to be loved by you, for you know how I think and you see all my flaws. You have allowed me to reach for the moon and have supported me through every success and mistake for the past 28 years. Thank you for allowing me to be on your team, for standing by me and with me, and for bringing such joy to my life. I need you beside me and am so grateful God brought us— and has kept us—together.

Marija: you are my gift from God, my miracle baby. Before you were born, I loved you; and the minute you arrived, I would have died for you. I thank God every day for lending you to me. While I've tried to teach you all about life, you've taught me what life is all about. You are the only person who knows what my heart sounds like from the inside. Thank you for gracing my life and allowing me to be your mama.

Mom, my angel: without your support, inspiration, and love, I would never have survived. You were the silent whisper in my ear when I was going down the wrong path. You were the one who taught me to trust in God and allow Him to guide my life. You taught me the Golden Rule and to pray on my hands and knees at my bedside every night. You are the place I came from, the first map I followed. I am forever grateful that God chose you to be my mom. I miss you *so* much and wish I had just one more moment to tell you this in person.

Table of Contents

Acknowledgments

I would like to express my gratitude to the many people who saw me through this book:

My husband Scott, for his continual love and support. You are the light of my life, my rock, my safe place.

My mother, because without her none of this would have been possible. She was and forever will be the angel who guided me through childhood with grace, hope, and dignity.

My daughter Marija Christine, my gift from God. You have supported and encouraged me throughout this journey. You will forever be my biggest accomplishment in life.

Attorney David Gibbs III, president and chief legal counsel of the National Center for Life and Liberty (NCLL), for encouraging me to publish this book.

Katie McCoy, my ghost writer, for spending her Saturday mornings with me for 15 months, listening to my stories of struggle and redemption, and for helping me articulate the lessons I've learned along the way.

Attorney Rebecca Dye, senior editor for the NCLL, for the many long hours of work to see this book to completion.

"For I know the plans I have for you," says the Lord.
"They are plans for good and not for disaster,
to give you a future and a hope."
—Jeremiah 29:11

Introduction

I'm not sure what made you pick up this little book, but I don't think for a second that it was an accident. I don't know what your background is, but I believe that somewhere in these pages, you'll discover something that inspires and motivates you.

The reason for this book is simple: my life is "Exhibit A" to what God can do when someone is willing to work hard and trust her future to Him. I had every reason to be a failure, but God had other plans. These are the life lessons I've learned along the way.

I've stumbled and tumbled many times. I know I have sinned, and I have asked for forgiveness. I believe Jesus died for my sins and rose from the dead. I have asked Him to guide my life and help me to do His will. And I am blessed beyond belief.

Many people know my name, but not my story. They've heard what I've done, but they truly do not know what I've been through. Their perception of me is their reality. I hope this book changes that perception.

The life lessons contained within these pages detail how I've learned to see my past as a stepping-stone rather than a stumbling-block to my future. I hope that by reading my story, you will learn to see your past—no matter where you came from or what you have done—in the same way.

Chapter 1
Your Attitude Is a Choice

94,000 employees—this year there are 24 "Chairman's Awards." One of those awards goes to...Cindy McPherson!

Had you told me that I would be receiving an award—let alone such a prestigious one—from the Fortune 500 company I worked for, I wouldn't have believed you. It was a huge honor. And it came at no small sacrifice. In 2010, the company issued a voluntary recall of one of our products. Every retail store, from Bob's Bait Shop to Walmart, had to remove every one of these products from every store shelf nationwide.

When a company issues a voluntary recall, typically all you as the customer see are the shelves being cleared in the stores. What you don't see is a fleet of sales representatives combing the nation for every nook and cranny where that product might still be available for sale. And what you definitely don't see is a customer vice president of retail operations overseeing the massive, military-like operation, managing the regional sales teams, fielding phone calls from company public relations personnel, and giving frequent updates to the president and senior executives. That was me: the customer vice president of retail operations, overseeing what would be remembered as one of the greatest crises in the organization's history. When the FDA broke the news that we were voluntarily recalling the product, the company president looked at me and told me that we would—without question—have that product off the shelves immediately. After flying to the branch office in Columbus, Ohio, which acted as the "command center" for the entire operation, I spent the next three weeks answering a continual stream of emails and phone calls. During the recall, I ran on fumes, averaging about 4 hours of sleep each night. Amazingly, we managed to pull off flawless retail execution in 59,000 stores—in just ten days.

The stress of the recall was enough to make anyone want to have a meltdown. I had stepped into an arena in which I had no prior experience, but not one for which I was unprepared. Yet no one knew what I had been drawing from to accomplish it. They had no idea what had brought me to the place where I was able to put on a positive face during this crisis.

What they didn't know was that this calm and composed woman used to be a little girl who had learned to mask her pain with a veneer of confidence, a little girl who had figured out how to tiptoe around chaos at home to avoid being beaten. No one knew that at a young age, I had learned to shoulder the weight of added responsibility just so I could have some order in my life. Many years before, I had figured out how to cope with the daily drama by putting on a happy face and not giving the slightest impression that anything was wrong.

I spent much of my childhood and adolescent years feeling like I was dying on the inside, while attempting to make everything appear fine on the outside. It wasn't until I was much older that I came to understand that the pain of my past, which I had perpetually tried to cover up, was something over which I had much greater control than I'd ever realized: I could choose the extent to which I allowed it to dictate my future.

From the outside looking in, I had every reason to become just another statistic: an alcoholic father, a co-dependent mother, a marriage right out of high school, a divorce shortly thereafter, and life as a young single mother with no college education. I believe that part of the reason I did not become a "statistic" is that I did not allow these facts, while true, to define me or to determine the direction I was going.

From an early age, I believed that hard work would improve my circumstances, and it generally did. But as I got older, I also came to see that it wasn't hard work alone that mattered; rather, it was my attitude towards my circumstances and my relationship with God that would make the biggest differences in my life.

Looking back, I can clearly see how God has used my experiences, my pain, and even my failures to change and mold me into the person I've become today. I don't know, however, if He would have done this had I lived my life continually blaming others (including God) for my difficulties and my own personal failures. I finally reached a point where I realized that if I truly wanted to change the trajectory of my life, I could not be a slave to circumstances or other people. I didn't have to be a victim and live with that mentality. I became convinced that my attitude would set me on a different path than the one on which I had been raised. And I write this book today knowing how true that is.

Lest this come across as yet another self-help book, let me be clear: I couldn't have done any of this on my own; in fact, I **didn't** do it on my own. It was God alone who enabled me, protected me, and provided for me a way that kept me from becoming that statistic. I know that if it weren't for the working of God in my life during the early years, I wouldn't be where I am today. And while God has done an amazing work in my life, the reality is that no one—not even God—would *make* me change. He had given me a free will and I had to make that decision for myself.

I don't know what your past experiences are, or what pain you have walked through in your life, but I do know this: you can change. Things can be different. Where you are right now doesn't have to be the final "period" marking the end of your sentence. It can be a comma, the beginning phrase of a story yet to be told. Maybe you're a single mom, like I was. Maybe you're the child of an abusive parent. Or maybe you've hit rock bottom as the result of your own choices. Whatever your situation, it doesn't have to end there. God has bigger and better plans for your life. In the words of one of my favorite authors, Lysa TerKeurst, "What finally helped me get past my past was trusting God to use it for good."[1] God can turn your life around if you'll trust Him with it. But it all begins with choosing your own attitude.

I love this poem by Walter Wintle.[2]

> If you think you are beaten, you are.
> If you think you dare not, you don't.
> If you'd like to win but think you can't,
> It's almost certain you won't....
> Life's battles don't always go
> To the stronger or faster man,

---

1   *https://twitter.com/LysaTerKeurst/status/501474761223208960/photo/1*, accessed 3/26/15 (originally posted 8/18/14)

2   *http://allpoetry.com/poem/8624439-Thinking-by-Walter-D-Wintle*, accessed 3/26/15.

But sooner or later, the man who wins
Is the man who thinks he can.

I want you to know that I am here today as a result of God's grace and hard work. I had every reason to fail, to be forgotten, to be put on the shelf of life and never given another chance. But God had better plans for me. And He has better plans for you too! They may not come in the form of what the world might call "success." They may not look like a big salary or a huge house or the perfect family. In fact, they will probably be difficult and will require tough choices on your part; but in the end, they will be much better than what you could have ever planned for yourself.

Throughout this book, I'm going to share with you some of the life lessons that I've learned—many of them the hard way. They are lessons that have helped me break the cycles of addiction, abuse, and anger. They have taught me that hard work and perseverance can overcome poverty, that kindness can overcome insecurity, and that humility can overcome the weight of personal failure.

You too can break the cycle in which you've been living. But if you're already convinced that you can't break it, then you never will—unless you change that pattern of thinking. I am here to tell you that there's a new start waiting for you. You don't have to stay where you are. But the success or failure of that start is largely dependent upon your attitude toward God, others, yourself, and your circumstances. And since your attitude is a choice, let me challenge you to choose well and choose wisely.

Chapter 2
Remembering Where You Came From

My fingers shook as I slowly circled the rotary phone and quietly dialed the number of the local police department. At just 11 years old, I had learned how to be silent. I was silent when I called the police on my father as he, in a drunken rage, beat my mother and my older brother. I was silent among my friends at school as I kept up the facade that I had a "Leave-it-to-Beaver" type of family. I always hated coming home from school; it meant that I could no longer hide behind the mask and that I had to go back to the world I tried to keep hidden. I don't remember the exact moment when I realized that my dad was always angry because he drank from those dark-colored bottles all the time. I do remember being 5 years old and slipping "happy pictures" under my parents' bedroom door when Dad was yelling at and hitting Mom. Maybe the pictures would make him happy, I thought.

I lived in fear of making a mistake. Or being blamed for a mistake. When I was four years old, my older sister and I were carrying groceries into the house and she accidentally dropped a carton of eggs. Panicked, she blamed it on me. Being the youngest of four children, and arguably the most precocious,

I was easy to blame. My father looked at the cracked eggs splattered across the driveway, then looked at me, enraged. I was too small, too slow, and too scared to run away. I froze in fear. All I remember after that is my dad picking me up by my hair and shaking me like a rag doll. To this day, I still have a little bald spot on the back of my head where he yanked out a section of my hair during that incident.

When I was seven, I was allowed to play with my friends at Silver Lake, just a seven-minute bike ride from our house. I wasn't allowed to go swimming, but I could get away from the house and sit on the dock with my feet in the water. One day, my brother, who was horribly ornery, rode his bike to the lake to make sure I wasn't swimming. When he saw me with my feet touching the water, he rode home and told my dad that I had gone swimming. By the time I made it back home, my father was raging out of control over what my brother had told him. He picked me up by my bathing suit, ripping it off of me. He then got the scissors, cut my bathing suit to shreds, and beat me with his belt. I remember just sitting there, so scared and so angry. I wanted to scream at him for what he had just done to me but knew I couldn't, for fear of what else he might do.

The previous stories exemplify much of my life growing up. I lived in fear—so much so, that at 11 years old, I wanted it all to end. I remember wanting to drink Clorox and die. It was a feeling of total desperation. I just wanted everyone to be safe and to stop yelling. There was but one—just one—redeeming part of my childhood.

My mother was my angel. She truly was my saving grace. A woman of faith, she exemplified unconditional love and unbreakable hope. She took us to church and taught us to pray and thank God for what we had—a roof over our heads and food on the table, which was more than what many people had. Mom was raised Catholic and believed that it was part of her "Christian duty" to remain in her abusive home rather than to seek out help. Tragically, this was an all-too-common misbelief during her generation, and many families suffered in silence because of it. While I'll never know exactly what she was taught that made her believe this and why she chose to stay with my father, I do know that my mother instilled within me a belief in God that has stuck with me throughout my life.

When my mom was 16, she quit school, went to work, and then married my dad at 19. She wanted children, but my dad was always so selfish and aloof that he really didn't want to share my mom with anyone, including the four children they later had. My parents so typified the addict-codependent relationship that psychologists probably could have spotted it miles away. He would beat her, she would make excuses for him, and then he would buy her something extravagant like diamond earrings. My mother was draped in diamonds! He would buy things for us children, too. It was like he thought he could buy our forgiveness and love. As a result of this unceasing pattern, our family lived in chronic debt. Every Christmas, he would buy us so many presents that it took him the whole next year to pay off the bill. This behavior wasn't only for the purpose of making unspoken apologies, though. It was just as much about keeping up appearances. Though my parents worked only modest, low-paying jobs, we still had a brand-new car every two years. Unsurprisingly, our family's income never came close to meeting our expenses.

It wasn't until I was in my forties that I first shared my childhood experiences with my friends. I had become so accustomed to acting like everything was fine. I felt as though everything would come crashing down unless I put on the mask of a perfect family. My home life was so embarrassing and shameful that I didn't want anyone to know who I really was. The first person to see that side of me was my first husband, who got me out of all that mess.

I understand what it's like to try hiding something that you just don't want to acknowledge. It seems easier to keep that mask on and give the appearance of a perfect, pain-free life. But that's all it is—a mask. Before I could ever be free from the chains of my past, I had to come face-to-face with it. That meant I had to admit to myself and others that I didn't have a perfect life, and that many of my own actions and reactions were learned responses I had developed as ways to deal with the pain of my childhood. For so long, I had lived in denial and was unwilling to face reality. Over time, however, I've learned a simple, yet profound truth: it's impossible to change or leave something behind if you refuse to admit that it exists.

It was only after I began this process of acknowledging the truth of my past that I was finally able to break free from the cycle of my dad's control. Even right up to his death, he tried to manipulate and control me, to make my life a circus of chaos. I had poured out my time and energy to help him and Mom live out their last years in comfort. I moved them five times and made sure they had what they needed. While my brother and sister lived only three miles away from them, I was the one who flew into town to help them pack their house. Yet my dad always repaid me with venom and paranoia. Shortly after one of these moves, he accused me of stealing from and trying to cheat him. I'll never forget telling him that although he had controlled my life for 43 years, he was done. I wasn't resentful—just resolved.

I've forgiven my dad, something I told him before he died. But I would never have gotten to that place of quiet, confident resolve if I hadn't been willing to admit to myself and others what my past was really like. Maybe you have a similar story. Perhaps you grew up with physical abuse or a personal violation. I know it seems like you're safer if you act like it never happened. I know it feels like you'll fall apart if you ever acknowledge it. But I can tell you with confidence that those feelings are lies. The truth is that there's freedom on the other side. Until you release the secret and quit hiding it—even from yourself—it will control you in ways you can't even see. No matter what happened or how bad it is, acknowledging it is the first step to breaking its hold on you.

I don't share all of these painful things so you will feel bad for me. I'm not trying to wallow in my past or complain about my childhood, but I do want you to know where I've come from. For all of the pain they caused, God gave me my parents for a reason. I've seen how my experiences under their roof—both positive and negative—translate to life lessons I've carried with me into the corporate world and in my life as a wife and mother. The toughest of those lessons was acknowledging the reality of my past—admitting that it actually did happen. I believe this was so hard because it was the first step, and first steps are usually the most difficult to take.

If you're struggling with an issue from your past, let me encourage you to take that first step. Be honest with yourself and others about what you've been through and stop pretending it doesn't exist. You don't have to let it define you and you don't have to be a victim to it. Simply accept that it has happened and confront it head on. Once you take this step, I can honestly say that you will experience a level of freedom you've never had before. Why? Because the truth really does set you free.

Chapter 3
Embracing Rock Bottom

I still remember the red velour seats of my 1980 Chevy Citation. Tears were streaming down my face. Marija was asleep in the backseat. It was time to leave. No one gets married and plans to divorce. But that's exactly what I was doing.

I got married at 18 years old, right out of high school. It was the classic "escape marriage." I wanted out of my parents' house. He was my boyfriend and a good guy, so we got married. For the first part of our marriage, we lived in the garage apartment in my parents' backyard. As much as I hated being so near my dad, I was able to be there for my mom. All my other siblings had left. From the time I was 13 years old, it had been just me, her baby, around the house. I was her sanity. She was still able to see me every day, which is why she took it so hard when we moved to Montana. The day we left, my mom locked herself in the bathroom, sobbing.

Our daughter, Marija, was 19 months old when we moved to Great Falls, Montana. From the minute my "Gift from God" was born, she became my whole world. Everything in my life became about how it would affect her. If I had ever needed a reason to break the patterns I grew up with, Marija was it. I had a new sense of urgency to right the wrongs in my life so I could give her a better one.

When we moved to Great Falls, my marriage began to erode. Perhaps it was because I was out from under the thumb of my father and, for the first time in my life, had some level of normalcy. I was beginning to experience independence and a newfound drive to do something with my life. I wanted to have friends, to have a life, to have anything and everything I didn't have back home. My first husband was, and still is, a good man, but this seemed to be more than he could handle. We were both young and extremely insecure.

Not long after we moved to Montana, I decided I no longer wanted to be married. Although I still cared for my husband, albeit more like a friend than a husband, I had been feeling like a single mother isolated in this new city. I eventually responded by doing the only thing I knew to do...I left. One day after work, my husband literally came home to empty cupboard drawers and a half-empty closet. I had taken Marija and moved out of our rented home to an apartment, just three days before our daughter's third birthday. The fact that I had really packed up my belongings and moved out without even having a conversation with my spouse shows where I was at that time in my life. I was unable to face reality and deal with my struggles in a rational, right way. I had never been able to do this; really, I'd never even had a chance to do this. To this day, I regret the pain I caused him when I left.

The day after I moved out, my husband walked into UPS where I was working. I wasn't sure if he was going to hug me or hit me. He calmly asked me why I had left and where I had gone. He asked why we hadn't talked about this before I packed up the house and moved. It was a painful conversation. We didn't yell or argue, and we finally agreed to finish the conversation after work that day. I picked up Marija from preschool and brought her with me to our meeting at the house. I felt as though having her there would help us keep the level of intensity under control, but the conversation did not go well and quickly became a heated argument. I got up to leave. As I did, my husband grabbed Marija, looked at me, and said, "I'll be here when you fall. You won't be able to make it without me." I can't explain what happened to me at that moment. Those words fueled me. They became my greatest catalyst for change. They somehow steeled my nerves and ignited a fire in me that changed the course of my life.

After our discussion, I sat, staring out the windshield of my car, about to be something I had never been before: completely on my own. From an outside perspective, I truly had hit rock bottom. I was 24, with a broken marriage, a three-year-old daughter, no education beyond high school, and only a part-time job. I broke down and cried, with tears of sorrow and self-pity streaming down my face. As I sat there, however, a simple truth my mother had taught me came back and began to resonate in my heart and mind—the truth that I would never be completely alone, because God was always with me. Although I didn't understand the Gospel at that point in my life, I still believed in God and knew that He was my only hope for change. So at that moment, I cried out to God in the only way I knew how: "Lord, please guide me! I'm not sure how to do this, but I need Your strength!" I told Him that I didn't know how I was going to make it but that I trusted Him. I poured out all my feelings and fears to Him and asked Him to help me get my life back on track. I believe God began, little by little, to help me get up from that rock-bottom moment. But it didn't happen overnight, and it didn't come without some very difficult and painful choices.

After I got divorced, my parents wanted me to move back to Minnesota. My dad even offered to pay for all of my moving expenses, but going back was not an option. I couldn't let it be an option because that was the last place I'd ever be able to change my life. I knew I'd never move forward if I kept one foot in the past. I could never give my daughter a different life while going back to my old one. No; this time, life was going to be different. This time, I was starting over. And I didn't want anything to get in the way.

During the next few months, I started to see that simply changing my outward circumstances wouldn't be enough to change the course of my life. I would have to be a different—a stronger—person on the inside. And God, in His infinite wisdom and mercy, began that process by allowing me to be tested in an area where I was very vulnerable at that time: my finances.

At my part-time job with UPS, we had several frequent customers. One of them was a local businessman who owned a bar in the area. He was a pleasant man and always very nice to me. One day, he pulled me aside and let me know that he could help me make a lot more money than I was currently bringing home. In fact, he said, I could give Marija a much better life than the one she had. He explained that he employed adult dancers at his business, and that if I ever wanted a better job, it was mine. Besides, I didn't have to stick with it forever; I could just be there for a few months until I got back on my feet and found something better.

I knew that I didn't have much in life. But the one thing I did have—that my mother had instilled in me and God was reiterating within me—was my self-respect. It would have been temporarily "better" to make a paycheck that I could live on without having to scrape by, but at what cost? I knew that if I accepted his offer, I would be throwing myself into a vortex of foolish choices. I knew I would go in thinking I was in control, but would wind up being controlled by that lifestyle. It may not have been a bottle of alcohol, but it would have been just as dangerous and enslaving as any other cycle of addiction. I also knew I would be disobeying God. In my core, I knew it was wrong. How could He bless, guide, and provide for me if I was knowingly going the wrong direction? I decided to trust that He would continue to take care of me. He did—in ways I could never have dreamed of. But much of that didn't come until later in my life—long after that rock-bottom moment when I sat in my car, alone, empty, and exhausted.

Maybe you've hit your rock-bottom moment. Maybe you're there right now. If so, I've got good news for you: many times, God does His best work in our lives when we are at rock bottom. When you're finally there, you know you've got nothing except what He can give you. And let me tell you, friend, that's the best place to be. Embrace your rock-bottom moment. Realize that while you are at a very low point—possibly *the* lowest—in your life, God doesn't want you to stay there. As the Psalmist wrote in the Bible, "I cried out to the LORD in my suffering, and He heard me. He set me free from all my fears." (Psalm 34:6). Your greatest failure and lowest point—your rock-bottom moment—may very well be the precise time and place God is choosing to begin a great work in you…if you are willing to humble yourself and allow Him to start the process.

Chapter 4
The Power of Influence

There's an old adage that says, "Show me your friends, and I'll show you your future." While this can apply to every person, it is perhaps especially true for those who are attempting to break out of the patterns they've been living in to carve out a new future for themselves. The people you let into your life will either help you or hinder you. It really does matter who your friends are. In my life, I saw this principle in action through a new friend of mine.

It was a very vulnerable time in my life. I had just ventured out into life as a single mom. Not only was I newly-divorced and needing to support my toddler-aged daughter and myself, I was living in what was still a new city to me. I was alone. Completely alone. Aside from the long phone calls I had with my mom, I had no one to talk to.

Except for this one friend. She had a little boy one year older than Marija. We had both grown up in the Midwest, with multiple siblings—she, the oldest of three, and I, the youngest of four. She was a few years younger than me but had very different goals, wants, needs, and values. From the outside looking in, she looked happy and content with her life. But, as I came to learn, this was far from the truth. She was miserable in her marriage, angry that she had gotten pregnant out of wedlock at a young age, and resentful that she felt like she had to get married because of it. She was constantly yelling and screaming at her son, and would forcefully spank him in public. She was very disrespectful to her husband and generally unhappy with life. Shortly after my divorce, she and her husband also divorced. Within a few short months, we were walking through the same challenges at the same time.

But we were not walking the same direction at all. During her divorce, she spiraled out of control. She turned to drinking, smoking, and late nights/early mornings with random people. I saw her going down the very path from which I was running. It terrified me because the truth is that I wasn't any stronger than she was, and I was certainly no better. I understood the despair that led her to those choices, but I knew that if I was going to change the course of my life, I couldn't go that same direction. It would have been a short trip to total self-destruction. I began to take to heart the verse which says, "Walk with the wise and become wise; associate with fools and get in trouble" (Proverbs 13:20). I had seen foolishness personified in my own family. I wasn't about to set myself up for the same wasted life.

At this point, I had a choice. I could try to manage our friendship, telling myself that I would be different and completely unaffected by her choices. Or I could put into practice the truth of Proverbs 13:20 and avoid what I knew would steer me off-course. I knew that I'd never be able to change my life if I was being pulled back into the old patterns from which I was trying to break free.

To illustrate what I mean, let's say that you're standing on a chair and I'm standing on the ground next to you. Which would be easier: you pulling me up to your level, or me pulling you down to mine? The answer is obvious because of the law of gravity—it's easier to be pulled down than it is to pull someone up. This analogy is at play in our lives every day because of the law of our sin nature. As you and I make choices to leave behind sin and wrong lifestyle choices—as we step up to greater levels, so to speak—we simultaneously fight against the gravitational pull of our past struggles, our sinful choices, and those external pressures and influences that would pull us right back down. Unless we have built up our own inner strength—our own spiritual reservoir of right thinking and right choices—we are very vulnerable to falling, due to our own or someone else's weaknesses. That's not to say that we shouldn't be cheering on those who also want to rise above their circumstances. But there's a key word in that condition: they have to *want* to change. And unless they want to and are willing to take the hard steps necessary to change their lives, they will only pull us down.

I knew that hanging around this friend would do just that. It would have been easy to continue my friendship with her. It was comfortable and familiar. Not only that, she was my only friend. But realigning my life with God's path for me meant holding nothing back. There were cycles to break and patterns to correct. And it wasn't just my life I had to consider; it was my daughter, Marija's, too. Every decision that I made affected her future. Choosing to remove negative influences put both of us one more step in the right direction.

In the Bible, there is an entire book of songs called Psalms. It has all kinds of songs: happy songs, sad songs, songs that celebrate hope, and songs that cry out in desperation. It's one of the best places to learn how to talk to God and tell Him what's on your heart. The very first song in the whole book talks about the importance of influence. It starts out by saying that people are blessed when they don't walk in the advice of immoral people, stand on the same road as people going the wrong direction, or sit in the seat of a person who ridicules what is right (Psalm 1:1). Those words always stand out to me. ***Walk...Stand...Sit.*** It's talking about where we go and who we are with.

The people you are around will influence you. The question is whether that influence will be positive or negative. God clearly tells us in Psalm 1:1 that we will better off—blessed—if we avoid the influence of those who aren't following His way. This is especially true when you're trying to change old patterns. You must remove yourself from the types of influences and situations that would tempt you to go backwards. It often means making the difficult choice to no longer be around people you truly care about.

Does that sound a little drastic? You may be trying to hold onto some friendships, thinking you can keep their negative influence under control. But take a look at those verbs again: ***Walk...Stand...Sit.*** You might think you can walk with people who are going in the wrong direction and not be affected, but I guarantee you, your walk will slow to a standing around, becoming more familiar, and getting more comfortable. Before long, you're sitting down in the very things you wanted to avoid. It usually starts with us justifying things in our minds, thinking that perhaps what had seemed so wrong isn't that threatening after all. We find ourselves thinking, "It's just this one time...I've had a hard week...I deserve it." Sooner than you had expected, you will have gone further than you wanted to go and will be further away than you wanted to be. Influence is like gravity: it pulls us in a very definite direction.

My decision to break away from this person proved to be one of the best things I could have done for myself and my daughter. While it was by no means an easy decision, it was the right one. Proverbs 27:17 says "as iron sharpens iron, so a friend sharpens a friend." If the friendships that you maintain are not "sharpening" you, then they are likely doing the opposite: making you more spiritually dull and lifeless. That's what was happening to me the longer I allowed this friendship to go on. If this is the case for you too, it may be time to reconsider the effort you put into maintaining these relationships, and, frankly, whether you should be holding on to them at all.

It is vitally important to surround yourself with those who will help and encourage you rather than hinder the steps you are taking to make right changes in your life. These kinds of people may not always look like what you might expect. It might be an older widow. Or maybe a quiet lady in the cubicle next to you at work. Or, perhaps, that neighbor who always has a smile on her face. Sometimes those to whom God has given a great deal of wisdom are the least vocal about it, so keep your eyes and your heart open, and pray that God would give you one or two real, true friends with whom you can openly communicate— friends who will give you solid advice and who will encourage you in your journey to do what's right.

What influences in your life cause you to feel pulled off the right course? Are your friends helping or hindering you in your journey toward life change? Trust me, I know how hard this is. In fact, it's worse than that. It's lonely. And loneliness hits a deeper place in our hearts than "hard" does. There's something about hard circumstances that can galvanize our strength to overcome what feels impossible. But loneliness brings an ache that, on a good day, makes you wonder if it's worth it, and on a tough day, makes you vulnerable to some very unwise choices. Just know that when you've made the choice to eliminate negative influences, it will be hard. And it will be lonely. But it will be right.

Chapter 5
Freedom from
Unrealistic Expectations

They weren't leftovers. That little container of Kraft macaroni and cheese was my daughter's dinner. And my new boyfriend, whom I later married and am still married to today, was helping himself to a snack. He had just come to my apartment to pick me up for a date. As I walked out of my bedroom, prepared to leave, I looked over to find him scooping out the last third of the yellow-stained noodles. I stopped dead in my tracks. He had no idea that he had just eaten my daughter's dinner. He had no idea that now I somehow had to provide another meal that I wasn't planning on, and one for which I definitely had not budgeted.

I had become quite skilled at hiding my financial situation from Scott. The truth was that I didn't have a spare dime. One day at the laundromat, Marija asked me for a nickel to buy a piece of bubblegum. I had to tell her no. We were that strapped for cash and, yes, every penny was important. Life as a single mom was a constant juggling act. I juggled all of the household management, caring for my daughter, holding down the best job I could find with my skill sets, and striving every day to carve out a different life for Marija and me.

I still don't know how I made it during that season. My first husband gave me $250 each month for child support. $190 of that went to Marija's childcare and $60 went to her food. I was working part-time at UPS, bringing home $107 per week after taxes. That gave me $428 per month. With $325 of that going to rent, I had $103 for everything else—utilities, my food, gas, medical expenses…everything.

Amazingly, I never went on government assistance. The truth is that I didn't even know there was such a thing! I guess that's how unprepared for the world I was. I remember my dad going on strike (frequently) when I was growing up and us living on food stamps, but I had no comprehension of how to even go about finding those. In my mind, I either had to live on $428 a month, or go back to my parents. And going back was not an option.

So I found ways to make it work. One was holding onto every dime. Another was buying those little boxes of Kraft macaroni and cheese. I could buy three for 99¢ at the local Buttrey Food and Drug store. One box would produce three portions. Those and one package of hot dogs would make nine of Marija's dinners. To this day, I can't bring myself to buy boxed macaroni and cheese. Just the smell of it sends me back to that time.

It's hard, thinking back to those days. Thankfully, Marija was so young that she doesn't really remember very much of it. But when I think of how we had to scrap and save, it makes me think of trying to run a marathon when you're knee-deep in molasses. You just can't move very fast or get very far.

If I could do it all over—if I could go back in time and talk to my 25-year-old self—I wish I would have asked for help. I guess that, in my pride, I was convinced that I not only had to make it, but that I had to make it all on my own. Sometimes pride can be a good thing when it gives you a sense of dignity and self-respect. But oftentimes pride can keep you from asking for and accepting help. My first husband's words lingered in my heart, that, at some point, I would fail and go back to him. I couldn't bear the prospect of moving backwards, so I just kept it all together the best I knew how. You know, the fake-it-till-you-make-it philosophy. I wish I had let Scott know the situation we were in. I suppose I was afraid that if he tried to help us, I would have always wondered if he had stayed because he had pity on me or something. I was already starting over with nothing. Had I admitted that I needed help, I think I would have felt something even worse than failure: I would have felt humiliation.

The truth is that I probably didn't have to hobble along on my own like I did. While I didn't go on government assistance, I likely would have discovered other opportunities for help had I confided in someone what my life was really like. I know in particular that Scott would have helped us during that season, but I was too embarrassed to reach out and let him or anyone else know about my situation. Since that time, I've learned that no one can do it all on their own. No one is an island. And while God definitely provided for me, I wonder if I kept myself in a holding pattern longer than necessary because of my unwillingness to ask for help. My pride kept me from seeing the wisdom of humbly letting others into my situation and revealing my vulnerability.

Maybe your self-expectations are different. Maybe you think you have to be perfect. The result is that you probably walk around upset with yourself or downright depressed when you make a mistake. Or perhaps you're expecting yourself to rebound from an illness faster that you really can, and the result is that you're frustrated and impatient with your recovery. Maybe it pertains to a relationship, an educational goal, or your job.

There is no shame in reaching out for help. It doesn't mean that you're less driven, resourceful, or hard-working. It just means that you might need a little guidance to get you moving along the right track. Starting over is tough. Starting over with nothing is even tougher. But starting over with nothing and never letting anyone in your life know about it is simply unnecessary.

Unrealistic expectations can quickly become self-defeating standards. If you're trying to change the course of your life and feel like you're not getting anywhere, perhaps it's time to stop allowing pride to stand in your way of asking for help. Are you trying to muscle your way out of your situation by sheer will-power alone? Have you been wondering how long you can keep it up, knowing that you're only one step away from falling apart? It's time to admit that you can't make it all on your own and ask for help. It's time to let your guard down. The thing that may be holding you back is you.

Scott and I married in 1986. Thankfully, I only had to endure that tough season as a single mom for a year and a half, although it was several years before I told him about the macaroni and cheese incident. It's a funny story now, but it serves to remind me that there will be times when I need to ask for and accept help. I'm grateful that God brought people into my life who were able to help me stay on the right track despite myself. And I'm grateful that I no longer try to live up to my own self-imposed, impossible standards. If you're in a season of starting over, I hope you'll let others into your situation and release yourself from the very unrealistic expectation that you have to "go it alone." You don't.

Chapter 6
One Act of Kindness

It was, quite possibly, the toughest phone call I had ever made. I felt sick. The pit in my stomach weighed more and more heavily with every number I dialed. This could have been my big break, the moment that everything began to really turn around. But I had blown it. I had lied on my job application. And it was only a matter of time before it was discovered.

While working at UPS, I met the owner of Montana Food Brokers, who offered me a part time merchandising position working 12–15 hours a week. Since I was newly married to Scott and my daughter was starting kindergarten, this was the perfect position for me to make some additional bread-and-butter money. I took the job and was quickly promoted to a full-time sales representative. Eventually, they asked me to relocate to Spokane, Washington, to manage their branch office. Two years after moving to Spokane, the branch office was purchased by another regional food broker. Soon after the transition, I was promoted from a sales representative to an account executive. Four years later, I learned of a territory representative position open at a Fortune 500 company in Spokane. I knew I could do the work…but in terms of qualifications, I had worked only as a sales consultant for a food broker or a third-party sales agency. I knew that I didn't have the education this company's other sales representatives did. Me, working for a Fortune 500 company…could that be possible? I didn't have the education, but I did have retail sales experience. Would that be enough?

Tentatively, I started filling in the blanks of the application. When I came to the section on education, I just stared at it. How would a high school diploma from a barely-credible public education get my name anything more than a quick glance and a toss into the trash bin? I didn't have the education I needed, so I made it up. Under "College Attended," I wrote "University of Minnesota, Duluth." Yep…I lied on the job application— gave myself a degree in business, in fact. I still shake my head when I think about it.

Now about this point, you're probably thinking the same thing I did after I submitted it. All it would take is one phone call to the university's transcript office to realize that a Cindy M. Kokal with my Social Security number had never been in their system. I'm telling you, it was such a ridiculous thing to do that it's almost funny.

But dialing that number felt anything but funny. The guilt I had been feeling was horrible, so I decided to call the hiring manager and tell him what I had done. With my heart racing, I made the call. I was determined to make this right…especially before someone else discovered my dishonesty. The nausea built with every step. As soon as the hiring manager picked up the phone, the whole thing just spilled out. I have never felt so relieved! After taking a deep breath, I noticed he was quiet.

He paused for what seemed like forever. "Why would you lie about your education, Cindy?" he asked. Sheepishly, I replied, "Because I didn't think you would hire me after finding out I didn't go to college." His response floored me: "Cindy, you've been to the school of hard knocks...let me send you another application."

I couldn't believe what I had just heard. Was I seriously getting another chance? He had every right to be offended, to lecture me, to give me a "thank-you-very-much-it-was-nice-getting-to-know-you" reply, but instead, he was kind. Merciful, really. I had been given a do-over, a clean slate, along with a comforting dose of understanding.

That one act of kindness changed my life. I was hired, and within 18 months was promoted to territory manager. I continued to move up the corporate ladder, becoming the customer vice president of retail operations in 2008. That hiring manager had given me my break.

You know what's a little ironic about it, though? As hard as I had worked and as much as I had striven to be positive, diligent, and dedicated, my big turning point came because someone showed me kindness after a personal failure. I didn't deserve another shot. I didn't deserve anything. But when I was given the opportunity to fill out another application, a completely clean paper with no mistakes on it, I was given a gift that I did not earn. I was given a second chance.

It reminds me of Victor Hugo's classic, *Les Misérables*. A newly-released convict, Jean Valjean, was taken in for the night by a kind priest. Seizing the opportunity, Valjean robbed him of two silver candlesticks. When confronted by the priest, Valjean struck him and ran away. He was soon caught and brought back, but when challenged by the police, Valjean claimed that the priest had given him the stolen candlesticks. He lied. And he had been caught red-handed. This would be his certain one-way ticket back to the spirit-breaking life of a prisoner. But amazingly, the priest showed him kindness. He told the police that he had indeed given Valjean the candlesticks, and not only that, but that Valjean—his friend—had forgotten the other gifts of silver he had been given. It was a stunning story of mercy. From that moment on, Valjean was a changed man. He lived a life of honor, self-sacrifice, and kindness.

Although my story may not be as dramatic, I believe that God's mercy was at work when that hiring manager gave me another chance. I didn't deserve it, in the same way that I don't deserve God's forgiveness. Yet from that day forward, I quit seeing myself as someone whose circumstances had to be covered up. I started owning my life and my history. I believe I was able to do that, in part, because this gentleman didn't make me feel ashamed of it.

Never underestimate the power of kindness. That one second chance could change your life. And *your* one act of kindness could change someone else's life. When I think back on that day, I have to smile. I had made one of the biggest blunders of my life. But instead of writing me off, someone gave me a second chance and changed the course of my life forever.

Chapter 7
The Power of Letting Go

It was the morning of my in-laws' 50th wedding anniversary celebration and there I was, driving myself to an emergency eye surgery. What had started as a burning feeling in my left eye had avalanched into a life-altering medical crisis, a six-figure lawsuit, and an absolute nightmare. Let me back up a bit…

I shared with you how I've always been really great at keeping up appearances. For better or worse, I could put on a happy face and no one would ever know there was anything wrong underneath the surface. Well, sometimes that mentality can influence areas of your life that it shouldn't—like when the time came that I realized my need for glasses. I don't know what it is about that 40th birthday, but all of a sudden the 20/20 vision goes haywire. After 40, I was unable to read a menu and desperately needed reading glasses. I wasn't about to start sporting those right away, so I opted for the contact lens route. I wore one contact in my left eye for mono-vision, which eliminated the need for reading glasses. Although it took some getting used to, I eventually adjusted to reading with one eye and driving with the other.

Shortly after Marija got engaged, Scott and I flew to Florida, where my daughter was living, to meet with her and her wedding planner. At the end of our Florida trip, I woke up in the middle of the night with a horrible burning in my left eye (the one I used for reading). It was so bad that I clearly needed to see a doctor. At the time, we were in the midst of an employment transition, and I didn't want to pay out-of-pocket for an emergency room visit, so I waited until we arrived back in Denver to go to an urgent care clinic. When I got in to see the doctor, he told me that I had developed an eye ulcer (so painful!) as a result of the contact lens, and he gave me a prescription for an antibiotic and a drug called Proparacaine to use several times a day. Since it was a Sunday afternoon, he told me to call my regular eye doctor on Monday to make an appointment.

I called my optometrist first thing Monday morning and got in to see her immediately. I explained the situation, including my visit to the urgent care doctor and the prescriptions I had been taking. What she told me still rings in my ears: "Stop using the Proparacaine immediately, and I'm putting you on a different antibiotic. I want to see you back here tomorrow." After my visit the next day, she referred me to a specialist, who discovered that the ulcer had actually grown. Not only that, but the specialist explained that the Proparacaine prescribed by the urgent care doctor was like pouring gasoline on a fire. It had eaten away at my cornea so badly that he was concerned my only real option was to undergo a cornea transplant. After 45 days of daily appointments, numerous prescriptions, and a tremendous amount of pain, the corneal specialist sewed my eyelid shut for 6 weeks. This was necessary because every time I blinked, it irritated the ulcer, preventing healing. So for 6 weeks I traveled with tiny Styrofoam-like pads sewn to the top of my eyelid. Unfortunately, this still didn't resolve the issue, so after 5 long months of trying various treatments, we finally came to the conclusion that I was going to need a full-blown cornea transplant. Surgery was scheduled for August 4th—one week after a previously-planned vacation to Hilton Head for my in-laws' 50th anniversary.

My travel schedule for work brought me to Hilton Head the night before the rest of the family. Without going into too much detail—and please don't faint on me!—my cornea perforated the next morning as I was getting ready for the rest of the family to arrive. Fluid came rushing from my left eye. I covered my right eye and felt a sickening realization that I could not see out of my left eye at all. I quickly understood that I was facing an emergency. I took a shower, put on my makeup (I told you I was into appearances), and took a taxi to the Hilton Head hospital. They immediately referred me to a corneal specialist in Savannah, Georgia, 90 minutes from Hilton Head. I was alone and had no options other than to rent a car and drive myself to Savannah. When I arrived, I was told I needed an emergency transplant and that my surgery would be at 6:00 pm that evening. When the tissue didn't arrive on time, the surgery was pushed back a few hours and finally, thankfully, completed by midnight. If you've ever had surgery, you know that all the preparation time means no eating and no drinking—not even water! It was one of the worst days of my life.

The nightmare was just beginning, however. When my optometrist told me that I should never have been prescribed those eye drops, I decided to take that urgent care doctor to court. After a three-year case and a 10-day jury trial, the doctor was found not liable. And because of the laws in Colorado, that meant I had to pay all—*all*—of his legal fees. I found myself owing over $100,000, in addition to my own attorney's bills.

I was crushed. I was stunned. But mostly, I was angry. The more I had to deal with this, the angrier I became. After the initial shock had worn off, in a moment of reflection, I asked my husband, Scott, "What does God want me to learn from this?" Without missing a beat, he said, "Forgiveness."

What he said was true. And it wasn't just the doctor I had to forgive. I had been harboring an unforgiving spirit and bitterness towards several people in my life for many, many years.

I had to start by forgiving the doctor who had caused all of this pain. It took some time, but after much soul-searching, I did. I couldn't hold on to the bitterness I felt because I knew that it would eat me alive.

More than anyone, however, I had to forgive my dad for the havoc he had wreaked in my life. I began by writing him a heartfelt letter, telling him my true feelings about him and that all I had ever wanted was to be appreciated and loved. It was the first time in 44 years that I told him how I felt, with absolutely no fear of repercussions. In a sense, this was the beginning of my "letting go" of the bitterness and anger I had felt all those years. I sent him the letter but did not speak to him again until the night before he died, 10 months later. My parting words to him were "I love you." When he died, my aunt told me I should burn the letter—a copy of which I had kept with me all those months—with his ashes, sort of a having-the-last-word moment. But I couldn't do it. I cut up the letter. It was my way of letting it all go.

In a way, I had to forgive my mom, too. Not that I was harboring anger towards her, but I had to let go of asking why she never left my dad or asked for help, or why she continually enabled my dad's addictions, or why she kept her four children in a home where they were abused. As much as she was my angel on earth, I wish she had found the courage to stand up and walk out of that prison.

So how do you go about forgiving, exactly? It starts with simply making the choice to forgive. That doesn't mean you are approving of or turning a blind eye to the wrong someone has done against you. It means you are choosing to no longer hold on to it. It means letting go of the debt that they owe you for what they did or what they should have done but failed to do. It means giving that person, and all the pain they've caused you, over to God completely. And the beauty of forgiveness is that when you choose to let the offense go, it lets go of you. Lewis Smeades once said, "To forgive is to set a prisoner free and discover that the prisoner was you."[3] When you forgive, you let go of trying to get back what you believe that person owes you.

Noted motivational speaker Tony Robbins said it this way: "Forgiveness is a gift you give yourself."[4] If you don't like forgiving, join the club! Fortunately, feeling has very little to do with the freedom that's found in forgiveness. In fact, our feelings tend to follow the result of our choice to forgive.

Maybe this analogy will help you visualize the process of forgiveness: picture the offense as a fishhook which has sunk itself into you, causing great pain. The longer you allow that fishhook to stay there, the greater the pain and the greater the likelihood that you will develop not just a localized infection, but one that spreads throughout your body. That's exactly

3 *http://thinkexist.com/quotes/lewis_b._smedes/*, accessed 3/26/15.

4 *http://www.oprah.com/oprahs-lifeclass/The-Best-Lessons-from-Oprahs-Lifeclass-the-Tour_1*, accessed 3/26/15.

what unforgiveness does: if allowed to fester, it becomes bitterness and infects the body and mind of the bitter person. Now imagine, if instead of allowing that fishhook to remain, you remove it and give it to God. Now, the fishhook is out of you and in the capable hands of the One who is able not just to heal the wound it caused, but who will also deal with the offender and the offense in an appropriate manner. That's a picture of forgiveness. Instead of letting offenses against us bury themselves into our lives, we need to allow God to take care of the situation. Once we do that, the other person is in God's hands. Let Him deal with the offense and the offender. Meanwhile, we're free of that hook. We don't have to carry around the pain and the feelings of revenge or bitterness anymore. We can move forward with confidence, free of the guilt that comes from harboring anger.

Once we have made the choice to forgive, it is vitally important that we truly and wholly "let it go"—not just to ourselves and before God, but to that other person as well. Think of it this way. If you owed me $50 but were struggling to pay it back and I told you not to worry about it, you'd think I was pretty generous, wouldn't you? But if I continually remind you of the money and keep throwing my generosity back in your face, time and time again, have I really let you off the hook? The answer is no—not at all. True forgiveness means that I let go of not just the debt you owe me, but also of my right to keep reminding you or myself of it.

Forgiveness is a choice you *can* make, regardless of the response—or lack thereof—from the other person. It's a choice that is summed up well in the words of the former South African president Nelson Mandela: "As I walked toward my freedom, I knew if I didn't leave my bitterness and hatred behind, I'd still be in prison." Mandela's choice to let go of bitterness toward those who had wronged him created the catalyst for him to truly be free—emotionally—from the prison where he had spent 27 years. Regardless of what you think about him as a person or a politician, there's no question that Mandela chose to allow his imprisonment to become a stepping stone in his life rather than a stumbling-block of bitterness. Maybe you've been trapped in your own prison of bitterness. If so, it's time to let it go. Choose forgiveness and you will experience a depth of freedom and joy that you will otherwise never know.

Chapter 8
When Falling Feels Like Flying

I could have lost everything. In fact, I *should* have lost everything. It's only by the grace of God that I got a second chance. Throughout this book, I've been sharing with you the lessons I've learned as a result of what I've experienced and overcome. I wish I could tell you that all of them painted me in a good light. But I'm human. And I'm sharing the biggest life lesson of my adulthood for two reasons: to demonstrate how God can take your mess and turn it into your message, and to keep some of you from making the same choices I made. I had planned to be successful. I had planned to change my life from where it was headed in my younger years. I had planned to give my daughter a different life than the one I had growing up. But I had never planned to have an affair.

Let me stop here and say that this chapter delves into the worst decision I ever made. I was not living by God's rules during this time because I felt as though that would ruin all my "fun." This, of course, is basically the same lie Satan used to convince Adam and Eve to eat the forbidden fruit. In John 10:10, Jesus tells us that the thief (Satan) does not come except to steal, and to kill, and to destroy. I was about to destroy many relationships and be humbled both personally and professionally by my lies

about the affair. I wasn't thinking about anyone but myself…
and I wasn't thinking how the affair would affect my life
forever. I was allowing Satan and my flesh to control not just
my thoughts, but my actions as well.

It all began so innocently—almost imperceptibly. Scott and I
had been married for 13 years. By the late 1990's, we were both
climbing the corporate ladder…and we lost sight of what our
priorities should have been: 1. God; 2. family; 3. work (more
on this later). Scott and I had stopped connecting with each
other and, gradually, we just grew apart. Before I knew it, I felt
like we were just living together, sort of perpetual roommates
who paid the bills, raised our daughter, and sometimes took
vacations. On top of that, my travel schedule began to increase.
I was away for more weekends, attending more seminars,
meetings, and conferences. My career was taking off, and I
found more camaraderie and connection with my colleagues
than I did with my husband.

Then there was this man. He too was a manager at my company,
and we had been going on the same work-related trips more
frequently. He was a nice guy, and also married. I enjoyed my
conversations with him on our business trips. One evening, a
good friend and I were talking with this man in a common area
of our hotel. My friend left to go up to her room, and I stayed
behind with him. We sat there chatting for a few minutes until
I finally got up to leave. As I walked away, I inadvertently
brushed against him. He noticed it too. At that point, I realized
the trajectory we had been on. All of sudden, our seemingly-
innocent friendship became an untamed fire. I could have done
several things at that moment. I could have decided to be more
standoffish with him, backing away from his attentions. I could
have confided in my friend and asked for her help to not put

myself in situations where we were alone. I could have avoided him at work the next week.

But I did none of these. Instead, I allowed the relationship to develop and go places it never should have gone. We talked about our personal lives, our marriages, our feelings. We confided in each other the kinds of things that build emotional intimacy, which eventually moved beyond that to physical intimacy. I wasn't in love with him. But, to be completely candid, it was just easier to escape into another relationship than it was to work on the issues within my own marriage. I had no intention of having an affair. But, as my mother always said, "the road to Hell is paved with good intentions." I knew better, but I chose to allow my desires to take me down the wrong road.

Proverbs 16:18 talks about how pride comes before destruction, and a haughty spirit comes before a fall. Nowhere has that truth been more evident in my life than during the 13-month season of my unfaithfulness. I thought I could control it, conceal it, and contain it. It seemed surprisingly easy. Since my job required me to travel, I simply told Scott I had to be out of town. As a manager, I sometimes worked 60 hours a week, so I could just say that I was working late that night. For a while the forbidden was exciting. But as I later came to realize and fully understand, sin has a way of distorting our perception of reality. The longer we live in it, the further we will go until we find ourselves doing what we never believed ourselves capable of doing. Although the affair continued for over a year, it took but a matter of moments on a Monday morning for me to be jolted back to reality.

It was Monday, April 3, 2000. Someone who knew about my affair decided to tell my husband. Reading an anonymous note, Scott discovered that I had been unfaithful. It was actually a very kindly-written note that expressed concern for him and told him that I had been seeing someone else. I still don't know who did it, and honestly, I don't need to. Though it didn't seem like it at the time, this person actually performed an act of kindness to both my husband and me. Had it not been for the note, who knows how long I would have continued down that road. Who knows whether months later, the discovery would have ruined any hope of saving our marriage. All I knew was that I had been caught. And as devastating and humiliating as it was, I had never been so relieved.

Confronted with my actions, I confessed the affair to Scott. But that was only the beginning of a long and painful road. I had to confess to the other people I had let down. My parents. His parents. Even our divisional vice president, whose words of utter disappointment still ring in my ears. But the worst part was when I had to tell my daughter. Scott had been such an amazing father and role model to her, even though she was not his biological child. One of my primary goals in life had been to keep her from experiencing the heartache that I had known most of my life. Now my actions would be the cause of it. When I told Marija I had cheated on her dad, she was nothing short of devastated. She was a senior in high school. I had wanted her last year to be filled with decisions about college, the prom, and other enjoyable times, but instead, Marija was forced to deal with the news of my affair and the possible breakup of her family.

For the first time, I was seeing my pride face-to-face. I had been tremendously proud in my marriage, but it was all about appearances. Pride is truly the most deceptive, pervasive, and multifaceted form of sin. In fact, wherever there's sin, pride will be right there. Some even say it's the root of all sin. The book of Proverbs is filled with warnings against the slippery slope of pride. It says that a fool takes no pleasure in understanding, but only in expressing his opinion (Proverbs 18:2). That was definitely me: I was more concerned about my wants and desires than in what was right or wise. I thought I had my life all figured out. But my arrogance set me up for a very hard fall. In James 4:6, God clearly says that He resists the proud, but that He gives grace to the humble. Had I been humble and recognized that the struggles in our marriage were just as much my fault—if not more—than Scott's, I would likely never have wound up involving myself in that affair. Instead, I just plunged headfirst into folly, thinking that I had a right to be doing what I was doing because I knew what was best for me. My pride in so doing almost cost me my marriage, my family, and my career.

I heard these song lyrics in passing once, and I can honestly say the words are true: "Falling feels like flying until you hit the ground." That was me. I had felt like I was flying, until I hit the ground...hard. And when I finally stopped moving, stopped lying, and stopped making excuses, I began to feel everything that I had been pushing away: shame, regret, even astonishment at myself, but above all, the dreadful realization that I had set into motion things that would be beyond my control. I had the power to decide whether I would have an affair. But I didn't have the power to decide the consequences of my affair.

Chapter 9
The New Start
of a Humble Heart

Scott had every reason to leave our marriage. In a way, I had already left it; I had just been keeping up pretenses. After my affair was discovered, I was convinced that I had ruined our marriage past the point of repair. There was no going back. How I wished I'd had a rewind button for the last year-and-a-half of my life!

Initially, Scott and I planned to divorce. My wrong choices had left such a gaping hole in our relationship that we felt like we were past the point of being able to repair it. We discussed splitting everything and going our separate ways. The weekend following this discussion, I was in Columbus, Ohio, and Scott was in Florida. That Sunday, as Scott sat in church, reeling from the events of the past week, the preacher began to speak about...you guessed it...forgiveness. That was, without a doubt, a "circumstance" which only God, in His sovereignty, could have orchestrated. I say "circumstance" in quotes because I don't believe this was by chance, and neither does Scott. He could have stayed angry with me. He could have held this serious failure against me and gone ahead with the divorce. But instead, he chose to listen to what God was asking him to do and something that only God could give him the power to do: forgive.

At the moment Scott chose to forgive me, I was given a new lease on life, a new chance to make things right in the best way I could. He called me after church and told me he had forgiven me. We started talking about the things that had built up in our lives and had gone unaddressed. We started looking for ways to restore our marriage rather than to leave it. In a way, we started over.

We went to Christian counseling to begin the restoration process. And it was definitely a process. Our marriage transformation did not happen overnight and, at times, was downright painful. For the first time in my adult life, I had to relive some of the haunting memories from my childhood—things that I didn't even realize were affecting the way I was living. I started being honest with myself about the past and began confronting things that I had preferred never to visit again.

The Sunday after we began marriage counseling, I slipped a Bible verse into Scott's day-planner. It was a verse that I had been meditating on—one that had been marinating deep into my heart: "And you will know the truth, and the truth will set you free." (John 8:32). The next day Scott emailed me something that I have kept to this day. His words of grace encouraged me. He said that together, and with God's help, every day was becoming better. He told me that he knew it would have been more comfortable to avoid the truth and the consequences that came with it. He thanked me for being willing to change and to live within our marriage as God had intended. And he pledged his forgiveness and devotion to help me become the person I was meant to be, the person he had come to know more deeply in the last week.

If ever I had loved him, it was then and there. His forgiveness changed the course of our marriage. It not only prevented it from ending, but it provided a way to grow past my sin and my failure. It was a costly move on his part. He laid aside his anger, resentment, and pride, and decided not to hold what I had done over my head. There's a song called "Forgiveness" by artist Matthew West that sums up what Scott must have felt in forgiving me:

> It's the hardest thing to give away,
> And the last thing on your mind today;
> It always goes to those who don't deserve;
> It's the opposite of how you feel,
> When the pain they caused is just too real.
> It takes everything you have to say the word…
> Forgiveness, Forgiveness.

Perhaps you're like Scott. You've been betrayed and wronged by your spouse, and you have every reason to stay angry. Whether or not you have remained in your marriage, let me encourage you to forgive that person.

On the other hand, perhaps you're like me. You've blown it—big time. You don't deserve to be forgiven. You know and you see how your actions have really hurt the ones closest to you, and you're wondering how to rebuild. If this is you, the best advice I can give you is to humble yourself. Be willing to admit your sin and the damage you have caused, and ask for forgiveness. And then, be willing to accept the consequences of your actions.

As we walked through the painful process of restoring our marriage, God humbled me. I didn't want to miss any of these lessons, so I started a journal. I had never been really big on journaling, but it helped me chronicle where I was in the whole process. Restoration was a one-day-at-a-time thing. It took a lot of wrestling with the Lord and changing my perspective from one of prideful complaining to one of humble thanksgiving. I've included several of the entries below. I don't share this with you so you'll think that I'm super-spiritual—far from it. These journal entries are a testament to God's grace, love, forgiveness, and ability to transform. He did it for me. He can do it for you, too.

April 25, 2000: Thank you, Lord, for giving me the strength to tell all my fears and open my heart to Scott. I am pained with heartache for breaking up my marriage and for hurting so many people in the process. I am very thankful for your strength to allow me to heal from 39 years of pain. I know you will comfort me while I cry, wipe my tears, and love me to healing…and I thank you for that.

April 26, 2000: Thank you, Lord, for giving me the strength today to complete a 14-hour workday on one hour of sleep. Talking with Scott until 3:00 am was very therapeutic for me. The closeness I feel toward him is unexplainable and I respect Scott now more than ever.

April 30, 2000: Thank you for helping me to answer Scott's questions. I struggle with reliving all the details. I understand his questions are part of the healing process. I just struggle with hurting him over and over again. Your guidance has helped me to work through the details and allows me to table my frustration. I need your strength, Lord.

May 2, 2000: Thank you, Lord, for this time of forgiveness and reconciliation with Scott. I beg for your strength to work through our emotional days. It's always been my nature to run from problems. I want to face these challenges and not make excuses and blame the past for my terrible choices. I do not want to use my past emotional wounds as an excuse for my behavior. I take ownership of my actions in hurting Scott, Marija, our parents, our family, and our friends. I will not allow my past to determine my future.

May 14, 2000: Mother's Day— Thank you, Lord, for enlightening me today. I realize now that for over a year, I had been doing my own thing. I was living without guidance or direction from you during this time of my life that was filled with sin and deceit. Your love and direction have set me free. But my heart still aches for Scott, Lord. Why did I stray so far away from him? Why???? In these times of suffering, I don't want to turn inward to self-pity or outward to revenge, but upward to you, Lord. Please forgive me for my adulterous acts. I beg for your forgiveness. I beg you to continue to guide Scott to find the unconditional love and forgiveness he continues to show me. He knows that you intend marriage to be a lifetime commitment (Genesis 2:24). I truly love him, Lord, with all my heart and soul. I know you designed marriage to be indissoluble and I am committed to Scott forever.

May 24, 2000: What a difference one month makes when you have a change of heart and attitude toward life and family priorities. One month ago today, Scott and I planned to split our assets, schedule an appointment with an attorney, and sit Marija down to tell her we were getting legally separated. But because of your guidance and strength, Scott and I are back together and have never been more content in our marriage.

The genuine love I have for Scott is unexplainable. I am happy from the inside out for the first time ever in my life. Thank you, Lord, for showing me the way.

April 15, 2001: Happy Easter! The day Jesus rose from the dead. So many positive things have happened in the last year. I know that permanent marriage is God's intention. I can honestly say I have never felt this secure with myself and our marriage. I know Scott's love for me is truly unconditional. He has made every effort to forgive, reconcile, and restore our marriage.

No matter where you are and no matter what you've done, God wants to take you from the depths of your sin and failure and give you a new future. The cost of my pride was great and the effects that it had on my family were never worth the fleeting thrill of foolishness. But God, in His incredible grace, gave me a new start. When I was willing to have a humble heart, He was willing to help me. He can do the same for you.

Chapter 10
The Wisdom of Boundaries

There's an old story of a wealthy cattle rancher who had a beautiful daughter. When she became of age, it was time for her to go to school—a 7-mile journey into the next town. The protective father did not want his daughter to steer a horse and wagon by herself, so he sought out a responsible driver to take her to and from school. He put the potential drivers through one single, but perilous, test. He told them to navigate the horse and wagon safely past a cliff overlooking a 300-ft drop. The first several drivers meandered the wagon near the precarious cliff, each with success. The last driver took a different approach. Rather than approach the cliff, he steered as far away from the cliff as possible. That driver got the job. The protective father didn't want a driver who could get as near to the danger without falling over; he wanted the one who had the wisdom to stay as far from the danger as possible.

I share this story with you because I did not have the wisdom I needed to keep from straying near that cliff. In fact, my straying caused me to plunge head-first over the cliff. I don't want you to do the same. Since the affair, I have learned there are really two approaches you can take to boundaries: one is to see how close to the edge you can get without falling over; the other is to steer far enough away from the edge that you're not in danger of losing your footing. After I started rebounding from the worst decision of my life, I realized that I needed some trustworthy boundaries in my life. These boundaries now safeguard my personal life, guide my work life, and enrich my spiritual life.

God, Family, Work

I can't overstate how important it is to clearly define your life's top priorities. Being able to state in a short phrase what those priorities are will help you declutter the things that don't belong and will refocus you when you get off track.

For me, I want to make sure that I keep God first. That means aligning my priorities with what *He* would want me to do and seeing my world through the lens of Scripture. Keeping God first also guides me through challenging decisions in my family and work life.

My family comes next in my list of priorities. That means they get the best of me and always come before work. I wish I could say that I've always done this right. I haven't. I've had to learn to put down the papers, turn off my computer, and not look at my phone after a certain hour of the evening. I've learned not to send emails on a Sunday when the issue will still be there on Monday. We women are great multi-taskers, but sometimes we need to unplug, be completely present, and quit worrying about whether we're keeping it all together for everyone in our universe.

The greatest challenge I've had in keeping my family first is that I felt like I could never quit giving 100% for my job. I allowed the insecurity I felt from my lack of education to become a relentless slave driver, telling me I was only as good as my last mistake. I've always felt like I had to work ten times harder because of what I lacked. And, unfortunately, it's insecurities like these that have, at times, robbed me of true joy. But you know what I've come to realize? Twenty years from now, it'll be my family—not my job—that I want to spend Christmas with. It's a good thing to remember. I've also discovered that when my relationships with God and my family are as they should be, I thrive at my job! I allow myself to be "all there" at home so I can be "all there" at work. Plus, when I make sure work comes after my relationship with God and my family, I'm better able to discern when work-related matters really need my attention or when they can wait. When your priorities are rightly aligned, you can set boundaries in order to protect those priorities. God, family, work. It's so simple, but so important.

Nothing Good Happens After 9:00 pm

I'm a stickler about this one. The event that precipitated my affair began in a casual setting at a time that was way past business hours. Casual settings with co-workers or friends make it easier to "let your hair down" and relax. While there's nothing inherently wrong with this, it's easy under these circumstances to allow yourself to become a little too familiar with others. When this happens, it's only a matter of time before you say or do something that you'll regret. I once was eating dinner with some colleagues on a business trip. A friend of mine who was drinking started saying some horribly-insulting things to me about my family. I got up and left. The next day, he had no recollection of his words. While I could have filed a complaint against him for harassment, I opted not to and instead, encouraged him to set some boundaries. For me, those boundaries require that I remove myself from social settings by

9:00 pm. Think of how many careers and reputations have been ruined by what happened at an office or Christmas party that ran into the late evening hours. Leaving early enough lessens the likelihood that you will become overly tired or too familiar with colleagues or friends.

Accountability Is Your Friend

I wish I could change the past, but I can't. If I could, I would have made myself more accountable to others. I'm not talking about sitting down and confessing every bad thing you've done to someone else. Accountability is something much broader, like a wide safety net. One way in which you can be accountable is by putting limits on how and where you meet with co-workers or friends of the opposite sex. Do you meet in private settings, like closed rooms with no windows, or do you make a point of meeting in public locations like conference rooms, where anyone can walk by? I would strongly suggest avoiding situations where you're alone in a small space, like a closed office, a hotel room, or a vehicle. Right now you might be saying, "Cindy, this is way too uptight! I don't need these rules!" Allow me to speak from firsthand experience about the truth of 1 Corinthians 10:12, which says "Therefore let him who thinks he stands take heed lest he fall" (NKJV). It's usually when we think we are above making wrong choices— that we would *never* do such a thing—that we put ourselves in compromising situations. Learning to make the seemingly-small but wise choice of setting boundaries will keep you from developing bad habits that will eventually cause you to veer off the right path and go straight over the proverbial cliff. Looking back, it was unwise for me to have been alone with that man in such a relaxed setting. *It set me up to cross boundaries.* That's what these "safety nets" are all about—protecting yourself from temptation. You don't have to make a loud statement telling everyone where you draw the line. If need be, simply seek out a close friend who will help you remain accountable in those situations where you might be tempted to cross your boundaries.

Be Careful, Little Lips, What You Say

There will be times when you go to work, church, or a social gathering, stinging from harsh words that were said on the way out the door or still hurting from a conflict in your family. If you need to confide in someone, be wise and talk with a trusted friend who isn't of the opposite sex. Trust me on this one. When you communicate with someone about personal things, you're building trust. And trust builds emotional intimacy, which can easily lead to crossed boundaries. One of the things I saw in hindsight was how my conversation with this man gradually moved from professional to personal. I found myself confiding in him about issues in my personal life and discussed with him feelings that should have been reserved for my husband alone. Again, it's not about being uptight. It's about protecting yourself from building an unhealthy attraction to something or someone that would lead you into sin.

Let me challenge you to set boundaries tailored to your life. Consider the specific people you encounter and your own unique opportunities. Your boundaries may be different during various seasons of life, and you may need the help of a godly friend to think through this process. Taking the time to set up boundaries and consistently enforcing them will help you steer away from foolishness and will go a long way towards preventing self-imposed heartache in your life. You *can* avoid going over the cliff of personal failure.

Chapter 11
Living Out Your All-In Moment

There are sorrowful tears. There are sweet tears. And there are self-pity tears. I've never been a pretty crier, and the day I stood there in the ladies' room on the 5th floor at the Cleveland Avenue office building was no exception. I was offended. I was humiliated. And it was all over a silly earring.

It was 1998 and I had put my name in for a promotion to an open position as a district manager. It was a huge step for me, but it was coming at the right time, and I believed I was ready and right for the job. Along with feeling professionally prepared, it was a great time in my life personally. Scott and I had been married for 12 years, and my daughter was a sophomore in high school.

Now, some of you moms will know exactly what I'm talking about when I say that I was not about to be the *typical* mom of a teenager. I was going to be the fun mom. The hip and trendy mom. The kind of mom that a teenage girl would want to hang out with (I know I'm not the only one out there who's ever thought that was a brilliant idea, contrary to what all sound parenting advice would tell us!). One weekend, I discovered the perfect way to prove what a hip, trendy mom I was. My daughter and I decided to get matching piercings in the upper cartilage of our ears. It was cute. It was fun. It was a bonding moment. How much would anyone notice it, anyway? I mean, it was a small little stud in my upper ear. No one would even really see it…or so I thought.

That Monday, I came into the office with my newly-pierced ear. To my surprise, it was apparently about as discreet as a flamingo. My company's national sales director, who was my manager, mentor, and friend, noticed and, knowing I was up for a promotion, tried to give me some advice. Now, no one was in my corner more than he was; he had supported and mentored me more than anyone in my career. He said, "You want to be promoted? I would encourage you to take that out." I didn't think much of it. In fact, I thought he needed to double check that the calendar said 1998—not 1958. It was just an earring. It wasn't like I had dyed my hair blue. Besides, I wasn't about to sacrifice who I was for the sake of "fitting in." I had a right to self-expression, and my work-life wasn't going to control my whole life. So I left the earring in.

Fast forward ten days. The divisional vice president had just walked in and I was nervous. This was my big moment. But you know what's coming. He took one look at me and said, "You either take that earring out, or you will never be promoted." I was stunned. And terribly embarrassed. I walked into the bathroom, took the earring out, and threw it in the trash. That day I learned a very powerful lesson: whatever path you choose, you've got to be all-in.

Whether it's an educational goal, a career ambition, or the commitment to raise your children, at some point you will have to check your ego at the door and be completely committed. Goals that are worth pursing will almost always demand more of you than you ever expected. At times along the way, you will have to make difficult choices—choices that require sacrifice. When those times come, you can be all-in and look past the difficulty to the end goal, or you can complain about how hard things are. That's a very strong temptation, but remember this: you chose to be there and to sacrifice for that goal. No one forced you to make that decision. You need to accept what you can't change and do what you need to do in order to achieve that goal.

I suppose you might look at this situation and say, "That's not the way it should be. I'm not going to change for anyone." Please know, I'm not advocating that you should be disingenuous. And I'm definitely not saying that you should do anything less than what is honorable, honest, and right. But we live in a very ego-centric culture, and many people seem to believe that their schools or employers should adapt to or help them discover their own "true selves." We make work all about "us"—what it can bring us or do to help us. Certainly, you should find fulfillment in your work. But the truth is that, like anything worth investing your life in, it's not just about what it can bring to you, but what you can bring to it. And in order to invest yourself into something worth achieving, you've got to be all-in.

There's a verse in Proverbs that talks about not making a rash commitment (Proverbs 20:25). It's foolish to jump into a major decision or life track without considering what it will demand of you—what sacrifices it will require. Carefully considering the costs involved with achieving your goals will play a big part in whether you follow through with those commitments in the long run. If you want that promotion, you may need to adjust to a heavier travel schedule. If you want to have more time to enrich your personal relationships, you may not get to have "me time" in your off hours. If you want to stay in that better school district for your children, you may need to stay put in the job you have, even if there's an opportunity you feel perfectly suited for in a different location. Mark it down: whenever you set a goal or a course for your life, you will have an all-in moment. And you very well might have more than one.

For me, that moment was the choice to get rid of the earring. Oh, it wasn't just about the tiny little stud in my upper ear. It was about deciding who I wanted to be in my career and being willing to lay aside the things that didn't line up with that. After my all-in, earring-free moment, I got a few other things together in my professional life. I started dressing like the executive I wanted to be. I ditched the shorter skirts and cute tops in exchange for knee-length suits that communicated to my colleagues that I was ready to be taken seriously. I started presenting myself in a way that conveyed my commitment. And, thankfully, I did end up getting that promotion.

By the way, these all-in moments aren't just for the working moms and dads in the corporate world. For you stay-at-home moms, you've made a huge sacrifice. If you have the means to be at home and raise your children in this economy, count yourself blessed! There are countless working women who wish they could do the same. But somewhere between the dirty dishes, the diapers, and preparing dinner, you've probably wondered whether it's all worth it. Maybe you're thinking of how you could go back into the workplace and feel more appreciated and better able to use your gifts, talents, or education. Perhaps you've felt like other people don't take you seriously because you don't work outside the home. And that's ok. Regardless of your choices, your critics will always be front and center. Someone or something will try to make you feel like you're not measuring up—that you're making the wrong choice. It's important to remember during these times that your goal should not be to satisfy other people's opinions. You never will! When you've sought God's will about the issue, have considered the counsel of trusted friends and confidantes, and have counted the cost of the choice you've made, you can live in the power of being all-in. I love what Sheryl Sandberg says in her 2013 book, *Lean In*: "If I had to embrace a definition of success, it would be that success is making the best choices we can…and accepting them." That's what being all-in is: it's when we determine our goals and values, set a course for how to get there, and lay aside everything that would hinder us from that goal, including the opinions of others.

I hope you've come to a place where you have recognized the aspects of your life that are worth your whole commitment. When your all-in moment comes, don't choose the path of least resistance. Choose instead what will help you achieve your goals and don't look back!

Chapter 12
Letting Go of "Perfect"

Mark it down. Take it to the bank. It's a 100% lifetime guarantee. If you're trying to change the course of your life, this is a truth that needs to sink deep into your soul: it's time to let go of those behaviors and attitudes that you justify as "perfectionism." Here's the reality: so-called "perfectionism" is really nothing more than the feeling of needing to have absolute control over a particular area of life. But the truth is that you and I will never, despite our best efforts, be able to control every aspect of our lives. Why? Because we weren't designed to be in control. God is the only One who can lay claim to that power. The more we seek personal perfection in any area of our lives, the more frustrated we become, because what we seek is simply unattainable. Author Edith Schaeffer, wife of the Christian philosopher Francis Schaeffer, said it this way: "People throw away what they could have by insisting on perfection, which they cannot have, and looking for it where they will never find it."[5]

If you find yourself anxious, worried, angry, or depressed when life's circumstances don't measure up to your exacting standards, let me challenge you to recognize this as the sin

---

5   *http://www.goodreads.com/author/quotes/158440.Edith_Schaeffer,* accessed 3/26/15.

that it is and stop justifying your actions. The truth is that "perfectionism" in all of its forms and fashions is quite simply a refusal—intentional or not—to allow God to reign in a particular area of your life.

For me, I wanted people to have the perception that I had it all together. I wanted other people to *think* I had the perfect family. The perfect life. My daughter had to look perfect: her clothes had to be clean and coordinated, her shoes scuff-free, her hair fixed and always with a bow. If she was messy, I was freaking out. And then there was my house. Now, logically, you would think that as a full-time working mom, I would understand that something had to give. But that wasn't an option. My house had to be immaculate. If I had to choose between washing the dishes in the sink or spending time with my daughter, I'd turn on Sesame Street to keep her occupied and immediately clean up. I couldn't stand a mess.

It wasn't until Scott and I were in counseling years later that I gradually began to peel back the layers and understand that my need for control and perfection was rooted in my childhood circumstances. This realization was a very important part of beginning to overcome this struggle for control because it allowed me to understand my actions and the feelings that motivated them.

For as long as I could remember, my dad would come home from work, pick up my mom, and the two of them would go for a drive before dinner. It was their time to be alone. Nothing too strange there...except for the fact that my mom would always pack a cooler of ice and a bottle of brandy. As they were driving, she would mix drinks for him. He filled the hours between his workdays with alcohol. For our whole family, the day essentially revolved around my dad's addiction.

When I was younger, my older brothers and sister had to take care of me during these afternoon rides. After my siblings grew up and moved out, my parents left me at home by myself while they went driving. At the age of 13, I essentially became my parents' parent. I took care of the laundry. I cleaned the house. I made dinner. It wasn't just an alternative to running away or getting into trouble—it was my way of gaining some control. I desperately needed order. I craved structure. So every day while my parents were out beginning what would be my dad's inevitable nightly binge, I had a few hours to regain control of my life. Having dinner on the table each night and the house cleaned became a defense mechanism—it was one less reason my father might find to erupt. I was trying to contain his volcano of rage in the only way I knew how.

While this "need" for control was most definitely a reaction to my circumstances as a child, my choice to continue living this way as an adult was actually a subtle form of idolatry. Anytime we're giving first place or first priority to anything or anyone other than God—including ourselves or the "perfect" circumstances we try to create for ourselves—we are creating an idol in our lives. An idol can come in many forms, but it always starts in our hearts. It's what we depend on, where we look to find the solution to our challenges. It can be a relationship, a job, a bank account, a hobby, a feeling, or a "perfect" environment. Until we come to understand that God is the only One who can meet our needs and fill the void within us, we will continually fill our lives with idols that will ultimately leave us empty in our struggle to find meaning and purpose. I thought I could fill that void by creating order out of my circumstances.

Gradually, I have begun to overcome this perceived need for control and perfection. It wasn't an overnight thing, and frankly, this may be a struggle for the rest of my life. But the progress I've made has taken some serious soul-searching and confronting the memories that had a hold on me. I am thankful that God is replacing my pursuit of perfection and control with the realization of my need for Him.

Looking back, I can see how I inadvertently taught Marija to become a "perfectionist" (a controller) just like me. This is not the legacy I wanted to share with her. Many times during her childhood I would remind, nudge, suggest, motivate, direct, and (let's call it what it is…) control both Scott and Marija. I am grieved by how much I did this when I should have trusted God to be the One in charge. I imposed my own will in order to maintain control of every situation so that I would feel comfortable. I don't want you to make that same mistake.

As you have been reading this chapter, maybe the Holy Spirit has been pinpointing areas of your life where you have sought to gain and keep absolute control. Maybe there are areas where this is so prevalent that it is damaging your relationships. There's a good chance that those areas are exactly where God wants to begin moving—where He wants you to relinquish control over to Him so He can show you that He is indeed a trustworthy, good, and loving Father. It might sound cliché, but the truth is that when we "let go and let God" control our lives, we can really begin to enjoy the beauty and goodness of God's blessings, rather than remain miserable in our perpetual, failed attempts to maintain the "perfect" environment. God is all-powerful, all-knowing, and all-present. We are not. We would be wise to allow Him to direct our lives rather than continue in our present, frustrated pursuit of perfection.

Chapter 13
Choosing Life with Your Words

If abortions had been legal, you would have been one!

Have you ever had a moment when you were cut open by someone's words? It's the kind of moment that sticks with you. No matter where you go, no matter how many affirmations you receive, it's there, re-playing in your memory every time you make a mistake or become overwhelmed by a sense of inadequacy. It's as though your whole life could be framed in terms of that one moment those painful words were spoken.

For me, that moment came when I was 16 years old. My father continually made our lives a living hell, but nothing wounded me so deeply as that day, when, 5 or 6 hours into yet another drinking binge, he matter-of-factly stated, "If abortions had been legal, you would have been one." I was stunned. Paralyzed, really. I don't even know how long I sat there. Just numb. My own father had just told me that I was a mistake, an unwanted accident.

It took me years to overcome the lie that I was unworthy or deserved rejection. I guess for a long time, I masked it with an insatiable drive to achieve in my career, yet no amount of accolades could undo the hurt of those words or fill the aching void of self-acceptance. Ironically, even while I was striving to prove my father wrong, I was still being controlled by his words. That moment influenced my behavior for many years. It took forgiving him, replacing that lie with the truth of who I am in Christ, and creating wise boundaries between my father and me in future conversations before I was able to stop allowing that comment to define who I was and what I did. I wish I could say that his verbal abuse stopped as I got older. It didn't. It continued right up until his death.

I want to share with you two things I've learned about the power of words. At one point or another, you will be confronted with these two issues. And how you learn to respond will, in large part, determine the course of your life and the legacy you leave behind.

First, you can choose whether or not someone's words will control you. How much do we all wish that the silly line, "Sticks and stones may break my bones, but words will never hurt me," could be true, but we all know that it's just a tough-girl front for how painful people's words really are. You may not be able to control how someone's words hurt you, but you can choose the extent to which they will control you. As Eleanor Roosevelt is credited to have said, "No one can make you feel inferior without your consent."[6] I've found that to be so true. If you're carrying around someone's hurtful words, I've got good news for you—you don't have to anymore! You have the power to lay down that burden by rolling it onto God. Only then can you have the ability to hold on to what He says about you (Ephesians 1:3–14, Philippians 3:12–15).

---

6   Although some dispute exists, this quote is most often attributed to Eleanor Roosevelt; see *http://quoteinvestigator.com/2011/03/30/not-inferior/* (accessed 3/26/15) for a discussion about its potential origins.

Here's the second thing I want you to know: your words have the power to change someone's future. Proverbs 18:21 says that life and death are in the power of the tongue. Think about that for a minute. Your words can infuse someone with the energy of life or poison them with the rottenness of death. Proverbs 12:18 says that rash words cut like a sword, but wise words bring healing. Words are like seeds, in a way. Out of them can grow many different things, depending upon the kind of seed that was planted: harmony or anger, compassion or resentment, acceptance or rejection.

The next time you're irritated with a co-worker or frustrated at home, just remember that in that moment, your words have the power to hurt or to heal. Ephesians 4:29 instructs us on this point: "Don't use foul or abusive language. Let everything you say be good and helpful, so that your words will be an encouragement to those who hear them." Do your words encourage others, or do they cut them down?

I am reminded of an incident where I was guilty of *not* using my words to encourage. A few years ago, my company hired a new employee whom I soon came to suspect was not being entirely truthful in his communications with me and others within my department. I decided that he and I would sit down together and review his work so I could clearly establish what was going on. It wasn't long before he started squirming in his seat as he began to see that I wasn't so easily fooled. When I finally came to the conclusion that his work was not what he claimed it to be, in great frustration I blurted out, "I don't understand what is so hard about this. A monkey could do this job!"...Did I mention that this young man was an African American? As the words were leaving my mouth, I knew that

I should not have spoken them. I wished I could have grabbed them out of the air. But it was too late.

Now please know, my words were completely uncalled-for, but from my heart, they were not racially motivated. But he didn't know that, and it didn't matter. He filed a complaint against me and I had to undergo a full investigation in addition to sensitivity training. I learned a painful lesson that day: words matter. And before I speak, I had better make sure that I can live with the consequences of what I'm about to say.

An old preacher named Alan Redpath is said to have created this little tool that we can use before we speak. It's simply to THINK.[7]

T   Is it *True*? Is it accurate and right?
H   Is it *Helpful*? Is what I'm about to say constructive?
I   Is it *Inspiring*? Are my words uplifting and edifying?
N   Is it *Necessary*? Do I need to say this right now, if ever?
K   Is it *Kind*? Is what I'm about to say gracious and others-minded?

I try to put these principles into practice in my words. How many people in your workplace or church are carrying a heartache and just need an uplifting word? Probably more than we ever will realize. How often do you grumble or complain with your words? Perhaps you're stuck in a situation beyond your control and all you ever do is gripe about it. I have discovered that when you speak words of blessing and hope, and keep an attitude of faith, God will help you see the joy in your situation. Let me encourage you to choose life with your words.

---

7   *http://www.news-sentinel.com/apps/pbcs.dll/article?AID=/20141015/ LIVING/141019876/1008*, accessed 3/26/15.

Chapter 14
Smashing the Mirrors
of Insecurity

Have you ever seen those houses full of mirrors at a carnival or a fair? They're lined with wall-to-wall mirrors set at different angles, causing you to see yourself in different shapes. One gives you a smushed face, another a bloated middle, and another, legs that look like a giraffe's. The possibilities seem endless, but they all have one thing in common: they distort what you really look like. Nothing you see actually reflects reality.

I think that's a lot like insecurity. It's a distorted carnival mirror that doesn't reflect reality. The trouble is that we don't always realize that the reflection we're seeing is, in fact, a distortion of the truth. For me, it didn't matter how hard I worked or how successful I became: I only saw my lack of education. For years, I let that define how I viewed my career. I believed I had to work harder than everyone else to prove to them (and myself) that I deserved to be there. Plus, I was a woman! From my perspective, I had much to prove. It wasn't enough that I became a successful corporate leader. It wasn't enough that I did my job well. It wasn't enough that I had every right to quit "auditioning" for my job and to just start thriving. I believed people still assessed my worth based on my formal credentials.

The reality is that nothing could have been further from the truth, at least among the people whose opinions actually mattered. My insecurity was a carnival mirror, and it had to be smashed.

Whatever you've had to overcome and wherever you've had to come back from, don't be surprised if you find insecurity about your past nipping at your heels. It comes in all shapes and sizes, just like those distorted mirrors. It feeds off of your fears and grows from your self-perception. Proverbs 23:7 says that "As [a man] thinketh in his heart, so is he" (KJV). This verse is essentially saying that our lives will become what we believe about ourselves. Insecurities sprout up like weeds in the gardens of our lives. The key is to consistently identify and uproot them so they don't take hold of our thoughts and eventually exert control. We were created to know security, love, and acceptance. But our false beliefs about ourselves often keep us from experiencing those feelings.

How can we tell what our insecurities are? Most often, they show up in the way we talk about ourselves, to ourselves. I like how Pastor Charles Stanley describes it. He says that we can tell whether we have a healthy or unhealthy view of ourselves by our self-talk. For example, if you believe that you can't do anything right, you'll talk about yourself that way. If you believe that you're rejected, you'll start speaking about yourself as someone who is rejected. He suggests that the key to discovering your insecurities is to listen to the messages you're sending yourself: "[Negative] messages keep you feeling lonely, isolated, and unworthy. The only way to heal from their poison is to do exactly what you don't want to do—stop clinging to them, and bring them out into the open, where you can see them for the lies they are."[8]

What kind of messages are you sending yourself? Do you believe that you can't change, or that you're destined to repeat the cycles of your past? Do you believe that you're a failure or unworthy? If so, then now is the time to stop that pattern of thinking. Now is the time to smash those mirrors.

But how, you ask? It would be great if we could just take out a hammer and smash them, but it's not that easy. So what's the solution? Where do we go to conquer our insecurities and replace them with truth that sets us free and makes us whole? The answer is found in God and His Word. No matter what others think of me or what I think of myself, He loves me. My worst day at work or at home doesn't make a dent in my position of acceptance as a child of God. When I feel the need to outwork all of my colleagues, I can remind myself that I don't have to work for God's favor and forgiveness and I can relax in the knowledge that my performance doesn't define who I truly am as a child of God.

The Bible has much to say about the power of our thoughts. We really can control what we choose to think on, even about ourselves. Romans 12:1–2 tells us not to be conformed into the image that the world tells us to be, but instead to be transformed—changed from the inside out—by the renewing of our minds. That means choosing to think differently, choosing to think in alignment with God's truth. It's a process, and it doesn't happen overnight. But let me tell you, if you're

---

8 This quote and much of the preceding paragraph come from Dr. Stanley's *In Touch Ministries* website at this link: *http://www.intouch.org/you/bible-studies/content.aspx?topic=The_Messages_You_Send_Yourself_study*, accessed 3/26/15.

dedicated to identifying your insecurity and replacing it with the truth of God's Word, you'll find your whole outlook and perspective beginning to change. You *can* change the way you see yourself. It starts with choosing to listen to messages about yourself from the right source. Our own selves, our friends and family, and the culture in which we live will all too often tell us that we are inadequate. Only when we accept and believe God's view of us as His children will we experience the security, acceptance, and love that we're looking for.

I still have to battle with my insecurity. I still have to overcome the belief that I'm somehow less worthy because of my lack of education and my past. But by God's grace, I'm learning to smash the carnival mirrors of insecurity and replace them with a reflection of who I am in Christ.

Chapter 15
When Not to Say You're Sorry

Although this might be contrary to what you've heard or what you believe, there will be times in your life when you should not say you're sorry. No matter how people try to make you feel, what they think, or how they judge you, some things need no apology. It's a simple concept, but getting there can be a tough road.

I've shared with you how I had to let go of perfection and control in my own life. Had I kept up with that people-pleasing, performance-driven way of living, I would have been exhausted and completely miserable. Not only that, but I would have eventually hit a point of collision between what was right and what others expected or wanted me to be or do.

Whether you realize it or not, everyone in your life has certain expectations of you. However, some of those expectations are just not worth living up to. There's a spiritual principle at work here that's found in Galatians 1:10: "Am I now seeking human approval, or God's approval? Or am I trying to please people? If I were still pleasing people, I would not be a servant of Christ." (NRSV)

If you're determined to break away from the life you used to live, you're going to have to stick to standards that help you get and stay there. More than likely, those standards will make you different from your other family members, friends, and co-workers. It might be the language you use (or don't use) in the boardroom, the time you give to your family, the way you raise your kids, the boundaries you maintain in your personal life, the honesty you have in your business dealings, the places you choose not to go, and the things you choose not to do.

The reality is that you can't (nor should you try to) please everyone; you can't even make everyone like you. If you're going to make the kind of life decisions that put you on a different path than the one you've been on in the past, don't be surprised if you feel like you need to apologize for those changes. In fact, you should expect it. Perhaps it's part of your own growth. But the bottom line is that you shouldn't allow pressure to fit in or a false sense of guilt make you feel like you have to apologize. Even when you are judged or looked down upon for doing what you believe to be right or for acting in the interests of yourself or your family, don't get sucked into accommodating others instead of acting on your principles.

I'm not talking here about issues of preference. Of course we need to be gracious and willing to sacrifice our own comfort for others. We want to be Christ-like in all of our actions, deeds, words, and thoughts, and oftentimes that means putting the needs and wants of others ahead of our own. What I'm talking about here are those areas where you have spiritual convictions—those areas where God has burdened you with the need to hold fast to a certain standard. Be gracious, be kind, and be careful not to impose your standards on others or come across as judgmental. But be firm and don't apologize for your standards or for receiving the results of making good life choices.

It seems as though women especially have a tough time with this. In fact, the results of a 2010 study found that feelings of guilt are more intense among women than they are among men. The study also concluded that women score higher on "interpersonal sensitivity." Not exactly a surprise there! Women naturally tune in to the feelings of others. We notice facial expressions and tones of voice and a host of other things that go into interpersonal communication. It's what makes us great at what we do: we build relationships...we cultivate and nurture.

But like any good attribute, that sensitivity can become negative if it's out of balance. We can tune in to the feelings of others to the point that we feel responsible to fix them. And when we take on that kind of burden, it's only a matter of time before our personal standards collide with other people's expectations. Inevitably, we fail to live up to them and we wind up feeling guilty.

As you make decisions that you believe will further the goals you have set for yourself and for your family, don't back down just because others may not agree with you. Listen to good advice and godly counsel, but don't allow yourself to feel guilty simply because someone else finds fault or criticizes your decision. Ask God to help you make wise decisions, trust in His leading, and move forward without apology.

Afterword

Letter to My Younger Self

Thank you for taking this journey with me. I pray that what you have read in this book has challenged, inspired, and motivated you. As I come to a close in this project, I can't help but reflect upon how dramatically different my life is from where it began, and where it could have been today, if it weren't for God's grace. Reflecting on all of this brings incredible joy and gratitude.

If I could go back in time, I wish I could talk to my younger self and share with her some of the lessons and encouragement that I needed along the way. Here's what I think I would say...

Hey, younger Cindy. Yes, you with the broken heart and the bright-eyed ambition. I want you to know that it's okay to slow down and put the to-do list away. You're not going to fall apart if you don't get everything checked off that long list of yours. Having a clean house, a perfectly-dressed child, and a department store-styled self is not nearly as important as spending time with your child. Let me tell you something: it's time to embrace every moment and thoroughly enjoy it. You're so quick to move to the next task that you forget to really live. Take a step into the present, because, after all, it's a gift.

Be honest with yourself and with others because "the truth will set you free." There is nothing worth the risk of losing your family. Nothing. You'll have some falls along the way. What matters most in those moments is that you get back up. Your life is going to bring you some challenges and heartaches, none of which will ever be wasted! Don't run from them, because they are making you into the strong, confident, caring wife, mother, sister, and friend that many will love. Live life with an open heart and an open mind. Learn to let go of your failures after you've made right your wrongs. Forgive. Always, always forgive. Forgive yourself and others. And after you forgive, choose to forget the negative memories. They'll always be there, of course, but the only control they have over you is what you give them. Believe in what God can do through you. Remember that respect is earned, not handed out. Treat others how you wish to be treated and talk to others the way you want them to talk to you. Always tell your family that you love them and actively demonstrate unconditional love.

My dear reader, where you are today is no accident. God is using the situation you are in right now to shape you and prepare you for where He wants to bring you. Trust Him with His plan even if you don't completely understand it. And above all, remember that no matter what your challenges, failures, and setbacks, God's grace is always greater! If you trust Him, there is forgiveness and a new start waiting for you. There is unconditional love that's already yours. You can be restored. You can be whole. And you can rise above those difficult circumstances because God has better plans for your life than you could ever plan for yourself.